Why Do We Sing?

Miranda Nerland

Illustrated by Hayley O'Neal

DeWard kids

Why Do We Sing?
DeWard Publishing Company, Ltd.
P.O. Box 6259, Chillicothe, Ohio 45601
800.300.9778
www.deward.com

© 2018 DeWard Publishing

Cover and interior illustrations © 2018 by Hayley O'Neal

Printed in the United States of America.

ISBN: 978-1-947929-04-3

For Mom,
who taught me to find my song
and sing it courageously.

Singing is just one of the beautiful ways we worship.

We can praise God, learn lessons, tell stories,
and encourage others all through the songs that we sing.
(Psalm 105.2)

Singing is such a special part of our worship together, because every single person gets to praise God out loud!

Every mommy and daddy, every brother and sister, every grandma and grandpa and aunt and uncle and friend is welcome to join in when we joyfully sing beautiful stories about Jesus' life and God's goodness.

(Psalm 145.7)

There are
SO MANY REASONS
to SING!

Sometimes when you sing,
you are praising God
and telling Him,
"thank You!"

The Bible is full of songs of thanks and praise
because it is so easy to praise God!

He is good and fair. He is strong, and He protects us.
And He gives us so many chances to do the right thing.

(Psalm 59.16–17)

There are also songs that praise God
for creating our beautiful world!

God can hear all of His creation sing praises,
    and He can hear you praise Him too!

(Isaiah 55.12)

When you feel thankful about the things God has given you
or the wonderful world you live in,
you can sing a song about it and God will hear.

It brings God

great joy

to know that we are
thankful for our blessings!

Can you think of a song that tells God "Thank you!"?
Go ahead and sing it now, because God is always listening!

(Psalm 7:17)

Sometimes when you sing, you are learning lessons
and helping others learn too!

Since God made us, He knows that singing can teach us
important things and helps us remember things too!

(Colossians 3.16)

Singing helps us remember people who
did great things with God's help!

Like Abraham, Joshua, Daniel, and the twelve apostles.

Singing also teaches us to trust and obey God
and to shine our lights to others.

We can even share our feelings when we sing.

When you sing a happy song, you can cheer up someone
who feels sad or comfort people with weary hearts.

(James 5.13)

When you sing a song about Heaven,
you give weak people strength
and make scared people brave!

God loves to hear us sing.
He loves the sound of our voices
and the words we sing to Him.

He loves when we sing *loud* and *proud*
and when we sing *quietly* to ourselves.

The Bible tells us that even Jesus worshiped in song.
He knew that His Father loved to hear Him sing.

(Matthew 26.30)

God can even hear the song in our hearts
when we do not make a sound.

God loves singing so much that He wants us
to sing all the time, and He tells us so in the Bible!

You can sing when you are happy.
You can sing when you are sad or scared.

(Psalm 92.1)

You can sing a special song of thanks at home
that is just for God to hear.

i LOVe rOu, LORd!

And you can sing lots of songs with your family
and friends when you are together on Sunday.

(Psalm 104.33)

We sing all kinds of songs
when we worship together.

We sing *old* songs and *new* songs,
fast songs and *slow* songs.

We sing sitting down and standing up.

We sing songs that make us cheerful,
songs that are exciting, and sometimes
even songs that sound sad.

No matter what song we sing to God,
singing from our hearts
is what matters most to Him.

(Ephesians 5.19–20)

When we sing from our hearts, we listen
to the melody and to the words.

We pay close attention to what we are saying,
and we can always ask for help if we get lost
or confused when following along.

We don't sing out loud so people will look at us.
We sing out with joy from our hearts because
we want others to look to God,
and God LOVES to hear the special way you sing.

(Psalm 95.1)

And when we all sing together in worship,
we show that we are united —
that we believe the same things,
hope for the same things,
and trust and love the same God.

Our voices are all different,
but every song and voice is beautiful to God.

(Acts 4.24)

God loves singing so much that there is even singing in Heaven.
In fact, there has always been singing where God lives!
When Jesus was born, the Bible tells us that the angels sang
a very special song just for Him.

And did you know that God's special servants in Heaven
are singing to Him right now? It's true!
(Luke 2.13–14)

When we get there,
we will sing to Him too.

We'll sing brand new songs
that we have never heard before
and there will be many people
there to sing with us.

(Revelation 5.9)

We are so blessed to have a God
who hears and accepts our songs on Earth
and who is waiting for us to sing to Him
forever in Heaven!

DeWard kids

www.deward.com

www.ingramcontent.com/pod-product-compliance
Lightning Source LLC
Chambersburg PA
CBHW081252040426
42452CB00015B/2798